Rock Dreaming

Rock Dreaming

Poems by

Neil Creighton

Cover design by Shay Culligan

ISBN: 978-1-954353-31-2

Kelsay Books
502 South 1040 East, A-119
American Fork, Utah, 84003

For all First Australians

Acknowledgments

Many thanks to the publications in which versions of the following poems have appeared:

Around the Fire 6: Responses to Kanyinsola Olorunnisola's In This Country, We Are All Crossdressers: "Three Stories, Three Songs"

Poetry Quarterly: "Kyle"

Praxis Magazine Online: "Rock," "Beneath the Myth," "A Handful of Sand," "I Read of Massacres," "Rottnest Island," "Beryl's Story," "Tree," "The Vine That Will Not Die"

Verse-Virtual: "Boorimbah," "The Fallen Tree"

Contents

Rock

I walk past water gums,
roots twisting and flowing over rock,
cross the creek's eddy and swirl,
scramble up a long hill
to stand on a huge expanse of rock.
All around in the stone are carvings:
kangaroos, emus, women, men, shields, spears, a spirit creature.
Clans met here to dance, laugh, carve, belong.
I try to see them but only sense them dimly.
Their culture and songs have shrunk into the past.
They are now long gone.

I lie on the rock and close my eyes.
I am filled with loss for the changes of time,
for the tangle of history, for the injustice of the present,
the crimes of the past, its dislocation, theft and murder.
I know that where these long-gone people
once in such deep belonging, roamed,
my ancestors, England's rejects,
came from the other side of the world
and by force, took it as their own.

I begin the long walk back.
I'm thinking of descendants
now scattered in dispossession
through the land of their ancestors.
I'm thinking of a past that cannot be undone.
I'm thinking of a future still yet to be made.
I'm thinking of a great rock of truth
on which in reconciliation
we can carve old stories of horror.

I'm thinking of how this nation
can gouge a new and purer dreaming.
First stories must be told and remembered.
Then songs of new dreaming might be sung.

Beneath the Myth

The colonizer's justification
is neither veil nor deliberate lie.
It is the myth created so conquerors
can sleep easily in their beds.
So, the Australian myth grew
of a primitive nomadic people
neither owning land
nor engaging in agriculture.

Sometimes truth will out.
Sometimes stories extraordinary and disturbing
emerge from far beneath the myth.
I read of how the explorer, Charles Sturt,
exhausted, near death, labored
with his men over one last sandhill
to find a large party of indigenous people who,
though they had never seen pale skin,
well understood human need.
They cared for them, nursed them,
gave them a newly built dwelling
and fed them roast duck and cake.
Cake! That meant grain
cultivated, harvested and ground,
bound with ingredients now lost.
"Sweetest cake I've eaten," wrote one.

I read of how another explorer,
the diarist, Thomas Mitchell,
passed through organized towns
of more than a thousand.
Storehouses were filled with grain.
Women ground flour and baked.
Crops were sown in dry creek beds,
their roots seeking the hidden water.

Now I, whose heritage
is long centuries of warfare,
dispossession and accumulation,
well up with strangely sorrowing awe.
I read that their greatest achievement
was a co-operative system of government
and a respect for tribal boundaries
that extended across the continent.
What have we "civilized" societies lost?
Is it too late to learn from them?
Or must our individualism and greed
continue to ride a runaway train
headlong into the future's oblivion?

A Handful of Sand

On one side was a co-operative and sharing culture
much older than the armies of Rome or pyramids of Egypt.
Their various tribes were peaceful and stable.
Along the coast, food was abundant.
They went naked and unashamed.
Individual ownership or possession meant nothing.
Their attitude to land was much more than mere ownership.
They belonged to it and its hills, valleys and rivers
were spiritual objects created and shaped by spirit ancestors.
Their Dreaming was a landscape in which they existed
before their birth and to which they would return,
still in deep connection, at the end of their days.

Into this world sailed the other side,
775 criminal poor, their sundry guards, officers and marines,
leaving Portsmouth, leaving behind the smoke and grime
of their rapidly changing industrial world
and for eight months laboring on the sea,
crossing the Atlantic, rounding the Cape of Good Hope,
crossing the Indian Ocean and finally moving
between sandstone cliffs into Sydney Harbor.
They brought with them ideas utterly alien,
concepts of the individual, the primacy of property,
the superiority conferred by military might,
the assumption that the country to which they sailed
was terra nullius, land belonging to no-one,
and soon they brought all the horror of colonization.

Yet nothing stands still and eventually a nation
must begin to come to terms with its past.
178 years after the First Fleet a green shoot
emerged from the blood and dislocation of the past.

At Wave Hill Station in the Northern Territory
the Gurindji people went on strike.
It lasted 12 long years. They said,
We want them Vestey mob all go away from here.
Wave Hill Aboriginal people bin called Gurindji.
We bin here long time before them Vestey mob.
This is our country, all this bin Gurindji country.
Wave Hill bin our country.
We want this land; we strike for that.

Then a new Prime Minister, Gough Whitlam,
determined to break with the past,
travelled to Wave Hill Station
and standing face to face with Vincent Lingiari,
poured sand into his extended hand, saying
these lands belong to the Gurindji people
and I put into your hands part of the earth itself
as a sign that this land will be the possession
of you and your children forever.
A small shoot, still tender and vulnerable
but growing, steadily, year by year.

Let it flourish. Let it grow.

Historical Note:

On 3 June, 1992, nearly 20 years after the end of the Wave Hill strike, the High Court of Australia overturned the legal doctrine of terra nullius, paving the way for native title claims to land to which the claimants had a continuous and unbroken connection.

The quoted words in this poem of Vincent Lingiari and Pincher Manguari were told to the novelist Frank Hardy during the Wave Hill Station strike and were first recorded by him.

I Read of Massacres

When I was a child, I learnt the first Australians
built no homes other than simple gunyas,
temporary bark shelters propped up by branches.
Now I read of villages of stone and thatch.

When I was a child, I learnt the first Australians
were exclusively hunters and gatherers
wandering continuously through the land.
Now I read of storehouses holding tonnes of grain.

When I was a child, I learnt the first Australians
offered no resistance over land declared
"terra nullius," nobody's land, open to claim.
Now I read of brave Pemulwuy's twelve-year war.

And now I read of murders,
"forgotten" colonial wars along the east coast,
one hundred and fifty massacres,
maybe fifteen thousand dead.

I read of poisonings, planned dawn attacks
on unsuspecting, sleeping villages,
gun and steel against wood and stone,
more blood to add to history's dark pages.

I think of the pain of dislocation,
two hundred years of oppression,
of stolen children, stolen land, stolen hope
and the horror that hopelessness brings.

I think too of myths and lies told to children,
endless justifications invented and repeated
so that conquerors and their descendants
can live easily with their conscience.

There is no real ease of conscience in lies,
only the tortured twisting of the past.
Nor is there healing without truth,
nor reparation without acknowledgement.

What can we do now, we who for generations
have lived on land taken from others?
Now we also feel its deep connection.
What reparation for crimes long gone?

Knowledge of darkness can bring light.
Can light bring healing, help us be brothers?
From whence comes the compassion gifting us shared walk
through land once deeply stained with blood?

Boorimbah

Boorimbah winds through its steep-walled gorge
and then surges down the mountain,
carrying its story in rock-filled steps.
It tells of boundaries and belonging,
of Kumbainggari, Bundjalung and Yaygirr,
of their 60,000 years of belonging to country,
of belonging not in title deed or fenced boundary
but of belonging like the platypus swimming
in the clear water of Kangaroo Creek belongs
or the red-crowned eastern rosellas
in their surging, dipping speed of flight belong
or the mob of kangaroos emerging at dusk
to feed on the tender grass belong to the land.

There are stories it cannot tell
as travels first through cliff-lined canyons
and then finally in meandering patterns,
curling around its ninety-nine islands
before flowing through Yamba's high dunes.
The water birds rise and circle in raucous lament
but they have no sound for Boorimbah's saddest stories.
Boorimbah cannot speak of one hundred Bundjalung
massacred near the white sands of Evans Head.
Boorimbah cannot tell of twenty-three Kumbainggari
lying dead on the banks of Kangaroo Creek,
poisoned from flour laced with arsenic.

All's changed since those killing days
yet the river that flows to the ocean
still rises in the distant mountains.
and travels through country that once
was Kumbainggari, Bundjalung and Yaygirr land,

but now passing under long bridges,
passing towns with jacaranda lined streets,
passing cattle grazing in lush pasture,
passing the dense tangled green of cane fields,
passing fishing trawlers and timber trucks
and the speeding cars on the highway.
Everything changes but the river flows,
still carrying its old unreconciled stories,
still flowing past obstacles of denial and guilt,
still seeking an irresistible flow of truth,
still seeking to gouge a path of acknowledgment
straight into the heart of national conscience.

Boorimbah is the Bundjalung word for what the English called the Clarence River. It is in the region known as Far North Coast of New South Wales. Once it was thick with forests of red cedar. Now only a few inaccessible trees remain.

Myall Creek

9th of June 1838, Liverpool Plains.
Eleven stockmen ride into Myall Creek Station
armed with rifles, pistols and swords.

Thirty-five Wirrayaraay people,
elderly men, women and children,
are camping at the station for protection.

They flee in fear into a hut, pleading for help.
The station hut keeper, George Anderson, says
What are you gunna do?

John Russell answers.
*We're gunna take 'em over the back of the range
and frighten 'em a little.*

They tie them, old men, women and children,
to a long tether rope and lead them
to a ridge about 800 metres away.

There they slaughter them.
Anderson from his hut hears only two shots.
The rest are hacked to death with swords

Sydney Town and the rule of law
are 600 horse ridden kilometres
and an ocean of prejudice away

and although seven of those eleven
are eventually hanged in rare conviction
for murder of the indigenous

those some describe as white savages
rage in killing rampages
for another bloody ninety years.

Historical Note:

The Myall Creek Massacre was unusual in that seven of its perpetrators were hung. Whilst massacres and murders of First Australians were common and frequently caused official and unofficial horror, the perpetrators also had widespread support, and it is difficult to find any other example of conviction and judicial punishment.

Gifts

What gift for Lieutenant John O'Connell Bligh,
who walked through Maryborough streets
summarily executing First Australians?

What gift for Lieutenant John O'Connell Bligh,
who, from the safety of his boat,
shot dead exhausted, unarmed swimmers?

What gift for Lieutenant John O'Connell Bligh,
whose rampage was described
by the Maryborough Chronicle as

a blot so foul and deep-stained as will leave
on this otherwise fair portion of God's earth
the brand of eternal infamy.

Let Maryborough citizens inscribe their gift
for Lieutenant John O'Connell Bligh:
for services in suppressing the outrages of the blacks.

Let Maryborough citizens present
to Lieutenant John O'Connell Bligh
their gleaming, ceremonial sword.

Let the state later appoint
Lieutenant John O'Connell Bligh
a magistrate charged with administering law.

Note, however, how in Rockhampton
a gift came to him from horse's hoof,
blinding one eye and disfiguring his face.

Note also how some years later a final gift
followed long and sleepless nights,
an early death from an overdose.

What gift can we now offer
to those who still see Darkey lying dead
and Snatchem's desperate last swim?

Only this: our tears and grief
and our acknowledgement that we hear
our brothers' blood crying from the ground.

Rottnest Island

The wind blows across the dunes,
low trees and shallow lakes.
It doesn't weep or cry aloud,
but it should.

The swells roll across the sea,
curl in foam then slap on the white sand.
They have neither words nor tears,
but they should.

The luxury boats bob at their moorings,
and the restaurants stare out to sea.
They do not weep or cry aloud,
but they should.

Should they not weep for the 369
indigenous men and boys
perished from disease, malnourishment
or the cruel violence of guards?

Should they not weep for the 3700
indigenous men and boys
cramped in fetid cells now converted
to luxury accommodation?

Should they not weep for men
ripped from the karri forests of the south,
or the red soil of the north
and imprisoned on this low island?

Should they not weep
for these soft-eyed men
with their bleak and hollow stares
and for all the horror of humanity's history?

But always the wind blows across the dunes
and still the waves slap on the white sand.
They have neither tears to weep nor words to lament,
but surely they should.

Historical Note:

Rottnest Island is now a popular tourist destination a short ferry trip from Fremantle, the port for Perth, capital of Western Australia.

The Coniston Massacres

7 August 1928. Central Australia.
Japanunga Bullfrog killed dingo trapper, Frederick Brooks.
Maybe for sleeping with his wife.
Maybe for not paying her for work done.
Tribal elders, fearing reprisals, banish Japanunga.

11 August. Barrow Creek.
Constable William Murray, Chief Protector of Aborigines,
is sent to Coniston Station where he hears of the murder.
His instructions? *Deal with the aborigines as you see fit.*

16 August. Lander River.
Murray and his party find 23 Walpiri.
They shoot and kill three men and two women.
One of them is Marungali, Japanunga's wife.

17 August. Cockatoo Creek.
Murray's group fire on four, killing one.
They let the other three go, realising
they know nothing about the murder of Brooks.

20 August.
Murray finds four groups of Walpiri.
He says he is forced to shoot 17 in self defence.
The Walpiri estimate deaths at 60 and 70.

24 September. Broadmeadows Station.
Murray begins an investigation into a non-fatal spearing.
He and three others kill up to 100 aborigines
at Tomahawk Waterhole, Circle Well,
Hanson River, Dingo Hole and Tippinba.

18 October. Alice Springs.
Murray writes...*incidents occurred on an expedition
[where] unfortunately drastic action had to be taken
and resulted in a number of male natives being shot.*

Official records at the time state that 17 aborigines,
men, women and children, were killed.
The Walpiri, Anmatyerre, and Kaytetye,
who suffered the losses, say that up to 170 died.

Of that 170, how many of them even knew Frederick Brookes?

Historical Note:

Although there were many other massacres in the early 20th century, the Coniston killings of 1928 were the last.

The Fallen Tree

Hidden by reeds higher than my head,
a huge old gum tree had long ago
released its grip in the boggy ground
and fallen across the narrow swamp.
Now, every morning, my way
to the two-roomed weatherboard school
bypassed the mundanity of the road.
I ran freely through the bush,
past the smooth, pink barked angophoras,
down weathered sandstone outcrops
and over my secret bridge.
I was maybe nine or ten.

At school we learnt about indigenous people.
Aboriginal people didn't own land.
Aboriginal people offered no resistance to colonizers.
Aboriginal people lived a life of hunting and gathering.
Aboriginal people dwelt in gunyas.
All wrong, the myths of conquerors,
but the most wrong of all was this:
Aboriginality could be bred out in three generations.
Then assimilation would be complete.

There were no brown faces in our school.
Later, much later, I found out why.
For sixty years aboriginal children,
as a matter of government policy,
were kidnapped from their homes.
I ran free through the bush.
They were stolen on dusty roads
or on their way to school.
I day-dreamed in class.

They were denied an education
and trained to be domestic "servants."
I ran home in full assurance
that my parents were there.
Their parents were turned away
from locked gates, many
never to see their children again.
I suffered occasional punishment.
They were locked in solitary confinement.
I received security and love.
They were denied affection,
beaten and sexually abused.

There is no making amends.
Some things can never be made right.
When those first boats
sailed through the narrow heads
and dropped their anchors in alien water,
their cargoes were not just filled
with England's unwanted
but with the grief and ugliness
of colonization and dispossession
and all its concomitant,
self-justifying myth making.
Those old myths I learnt
as a child were not sustainable.
They grew in boggy ground.
They had to eventually fall.
What can come from their falling?
Could it be verities strong enough
to bridge myth's thick, matted reeds
and history's stagnant swamp?

Where is that place where all children
can run freely through the bush,
past smooth, pink barked angophoras,
down weathered sandstone outcrops
to walk together over our shared tree?

A gunya is a temporary bark hut.

Beryl's Story

*for all children of the Stolen Generation, and, in particular, for Faye
Moseley and Doreen Webster, whose experiences in the Cootamundra Girls
Training Home are depicted (with permission) in this poem*

I was only ten when they took me.
My brothers and sisters too.
We were walking to school.
First thing they cut my plaits clean off.
Didn't even bother unplaiting them.
Took my clothes and got rid of them too.
That was the end of school for me.
They said they were training us
to be domestic servants.
More like slaves really.
There was lots of abuse.
Sexual, too.
From the staff, you know.
There was also a tiny place
we called the morgue.
They'd lock you there if you misbehaved
or tried to run away.
Nobody ever loved us.
Nobody cuddled us.
Nobody praised us.
When they took us Mum and Dad were at work.
They told us Mum and Dad didn't want us.
Said they didn't love us anymore.
That wasn't true.
Mum and Dad had a letter
from the Aborigines Welfare Board
saying we were well looked after.
Didn't make any difference.
I found out later Mum and Dad

tried to visit Coota heaps of times.
They weren't allowed in the gate.
Dad couldn't cope.
He took off driving trucks.
Years later at Mum's funeral
this bloke asks me my name.
"It's Beryl", I say.
He says, "I'm your Dad."

They're still taking our kids, locking them up.
First inmates are always aborigines.
This is what the Stolen Generation
has done to us, to our kids, to our communities.

Historical Note:

The Stolen Generations refers to children taken from their families by the Australian Government between 1910 and 1970. It is estimated that between one in ten and one in three children suffered this fate. Its purpose was to breed out aboriginality through forced assimilation.

Kyle

for all abused and neglected children

Maybe his story was only half true
but he told it with such direct simple power
that momentarily the whole class went dead quiet
and through my mind washed
waves of sorrow and compassion,
a wish that over sad, complex, humanity
at least childhood could be simply joyous.

I punched me Mum so I 'ad t' bolt.
I 'id all day in a tree. I could 'ear 'em callin' me.
No way I wuz comin' down.
Me step-dad 'ud bash me.
Then I got on a bus and come down 'ere,
to me Ma and Pa's. They're awright.
Better 'n 'ome anyway.

He'd come from a long way,
big for his age, raw-boned,
a guileless, strange kind of innocent
always in conflict with older boys.
They'd veer to bump him in the corridors.
He'd mouth off at them, defiant.
He was only twelve.

Some years later I passed him in the street.
For a moment I didn't recognize him.
All that child's health had disappeared.
He was thin, very thin.
His head was studded and shaven.
His cheeks were drawn.
His eyes had that hollow, empty desolation
you sometimes see in those
who have seen too much

34

or known too much of human misery
and who have sought momentary respite
in a powerfully destructive vortex.
He was, I would guess, fifteen.

Finally, I read about him in the local paper.
A tide passed over me,
anguish for loss and waste,
for impotent helplessness,
for the misery of some children's lives,
for the blight that perpetuates abuse,
for those trapped in their individual torment.
He'd killed a man, a pedophile and his dealer.
Late one night he knocked on the door
of a house in a quiet sleeping street.
When the door opened he pulled the trigger
and fled into the night whilst those
in nearby houses slept peacefully on.
He was only eighteen.

I thought then of that quiet street,
of separate lives, of sleeping comfortably
in our separate houses and our separate beds
whilst young lives in agony of abandonment
flee headlong into the dark
and I heard the tolling of bells,
deep, sad notes ringing out
for every young and damaged life,
for every abused, abandoned and neglected child,
ringing out loss, waste, heartache, sorrow and pain,
bells echoing in desolate mournfulness
all through this dark and too often sleeping land.

Three Stories, Three Songs

I have travelled through stories.
In this half of the story the dead walk beside me.
I sense my mother's whispers, hear my grandfather's songs,
touch an emu gouged in stone, see ancient paintings in a cave,
feel primordial shapes labor from the sea.
Stars move inside me.
Earth is a pulse beneath my feet.
I own nothing, am part of everything.
To all that is, has been, will be, I sing
"Mother, sister, father, brother,
I am earth and to earth I belong."

Because *I have travelled through stories.*
I know the other half,
the one where I am trapped in dislocation,
where my tongue in confusion splits
and my tears drop on stone.
Alien gods close their ears.
My name is mocked.
My warrior forebears are ridiculed.
The land does not love me.
It slaughters my brothers.
There are no lovers to take me
from the edge of brokenness.
My father's ancient songs are lost.
Into the emptiness I sing
Am I nothing more than just
another consequence of conquest?

Because *I have travelled through stories*
I dream of songs new and old
where a different sense of belonging
is forged in anguish and tempered in compassion.

It embraces place, history and culture,
rejoices in difference, celebrates shared humanity,
touches, palm to palm, weeps for another's sorrow,
shares in another's joy.

Listen. Can you hear the music?
Voices in sweet harmony sing of new belonging,
a transcendent humanity, and the chorus is this-
beauty is not found in
temples and shrines but in the
home of sinful men like us.

Author's Note:

The lines in italics are from poems by Kanyinsola Olorunnisola and first appeared
in Around the Fire 6: Responses to Kanyinsola Olorunnisola's In This Country,
We Are All Crossdressers.

Kevin Rudd Says Sorry

They gathered on the grass outside Parliament House.
They sat in the gallery chamber of the House of Reps.
They sat together in rooms across the nation.
They watched the television. They waited for the words.
They wept. They cheered. They raised their arms in salute.
They reached out to comfort those who wept.
The pain of sixty years of government policy,
the forcible removal of tens of thousands
of indigenous children from their families
and all its associated misery, isolation and abuse
was being acknowledged by the Prime Minister.
He said he was removing a stain from the country's soul.
He said their stories cried out to be heard.
He said they cried out for an apology
and casting aside past refusals of less generous minds
Kevin Rudd did something for which the nation waited.
On behalf of everyone, Kevin Rudd said sorry.

Historical Note:

One of the first actions of Kevin Rudd's newly elected Labor Government was to officially apologize to those known as the Stolen Generations. This historic event occurred on 14 February 2008.

Booing Adam Goodes

The ball is in the air, high and spinning
towards the group of players waiting fifty metres away.
Adam Goodes leaps high above them,
clutches the ball and takes it cleanly down.

Scores of thousands boo in unison.

The ball is on the ground.
Adam Goodes pirouettes, surges,
shrugs off strong men and kicks long and true.

Scores of thousands boo in unison.

Adam Goodes runs with the ball.
Men fleet of foot chase him,
but Adam Goodes, tall and strong,
is too fast for them.

Scores of thousands boo in unison.

They are booing Adam Goodes,
indigenous footballer,
a champion of Australian Rules Football,
twice winner of the Brownlow Medal,
the competition's coveted Best and Fairest award.
He is also a social worker, an author
and Australian of the Year.
They boo every time he touches the ball,
and he touches it a lot.

This is what they say.

Aw, mate, it's not that he's a black fella.
It's just that he's a bloody wanker.
First he points out that thirteen year old girl
for calling him an ape. She wuz just havin' fun.
Then he kicks that goal and does a bloody war dance.
Geez, I ask ya. Deserves all he gets.
Wait, he's about to get the ball again.
Here we go. Ready, boys.

This is what Adam Goodes says.

That girl, she's young, uneducated.
If she wants to pick up the phone, I'll talk to her.
I don't think she had any idea of what she was calling me.
I don't want a witch hunt, but it hurt, hurt a lot.

The dance? I learnt that from an indigenous kid's team.
I performed it in indigenous round.
I was celebrating our culture.
I wasn't trying to offend or intimidate anyone.

They booed him right out of the game,
these ordinary men and women,
mostly good-natured, hardworking,
kind to their children, loving their spouses,
upright citizens of their country
but utterly ignorant of the long history
that made Goodes refuse to accept insult
and to find a way to celebrate his culture.
What did that crowd know of the Stolen Generation,
how thousands of indigenous children,
were taken from their parents
in a cruelly futile attempt at assimilation?

But Goodes knew.
His own mother was one of the Stolen Generation.

What did that crowd know of hidden massacres,
of cultural denial, of the cruel barbs of children,
of growing up a second-class citizen
in the land of your ancestors?

But Goodes knew.
He knew it from his cultural heritage.
He knew it from his experiences at school.

What did that crowd know
of his desire to instill pride in heritage
or his work for the disadvantaged,
of his desire to empower the next generation?
Surely, if they had, they would have stood
and cheered every time he touched the ball.
Instead, they booed this champion of his people.
Booed him right out of the game.

Sometimes, I hang my head in shame.
Sometimes, it's a poor fella, my country.

Tree

for Ikeogu Oke 1967–2018

Although they spread deep and wide
from before measured history,
these ancient anchoring roots
are still the one great tree.

Although it towers, twists and turns,
is marked and scarred for all to see,
this changing, gnarled and mottled trunk
is still the one great tree.

Although some bend to touch the earth
whilst others soar in elegant beauty,
this vast spreading tangle of branches
is still the one great tree.

Although they blossom, bloom and droop
in cyclical, never-ending creativity,
these flowers, fruit and seed
are still the one great tree.

So too we who dream and love,
who share the common bond of humanity,
who have hearts, minds, hands and voices
are still the one great tree.

Some branches may be full of thorns
but others grow in truth and poetry.
They raise their voice to sing
that we are all part of the one great tree

and in singing, rejoice,
in pureness of heart and simplicity,
across the deserts and mountains of this earth
that we are all part of the one great tree.

The Vine that Will Not Die

Here's to the vine that will not die.
Here's to its root, branch and leaf.
Here's to its tendrils of hope.

Here's to Gurindji strike at Wave Hill Station,
Here's to their spokesman, Vincent Lingiari:
We want to live on our land, our way.

Here's to Eddie Mabo's Murry Island landmarks.
Here's to his heritage, ownership and words:
This land belongs to me, not the Crown.

Here's to the justice of native title.
Here's to the end of land-stealing fiction.
Here's to the end of terra nullius, nobody's land.

Here's to the descendants of the Colonial Wars.
Here's to those of the Stolen Generation.
Here's to their survival and strength.

Here's to those who cannot be suppressed.
Here's to artists, poets, playwrights, singers, dancers,
musicians, sportspeople, actors, teachers, lawyers, doctors.

Here's to their sense of community.
Here's to kinship, sharing and family.
Here's to belonging to country.

Here's to people that will not be defeated.
Here's to the courage of common folk.
Here's to the champions of hope.

River

A dark river, often unseen,
flows through my country.
Once it ran red with indigenous blood.
Once its banks overflowed
with the tears of stolen children.
Still it carries injustice,
incarceration, deaths in custody,
the horror of hopelessness.
Still powerful voices continue
to speak out in ignorance and arrogance.

Yet it flows more cleanly now.
Heroes, too gifted for silencing,
have emerged from its turbulence.
Overflowing tears have brought
a counter-tide of acknowledgment.
Increased knowledge, like a cleansing filter,
has spread the gift of understanding.
What, though, can the future bring?
What can purify it or atone for it?
Can it ever flow freely?
Can this ancient land embrace us all?

About the Author

Neil Creighton is an Australian poet passionate for social justice. His work as a teacher made him aware of the horror of inequality. His poems often reflect his joy in the natural world, especially the creatures and places of his native Australia. Environmental degradation is becoming increasingly important in his poems. His poems have been widely published, both in print and online, most often in the USA, but also in Africa, India, and the UK. His books *Earth Music* (Praxis Magazine Online), *Loving Leah* (Kelsay Books), and *Awakening* (Cyberwit) were published in 2020. He is a Contributing Editor for Verse-Virtual, an online poetry journal.

www.ingramcontent.com/pod-product-compliance
Lightning Source LLC
Chambersburg PA
CBHW071751090426
42738CB00011B/2650